SQL:

The Ultimate Beginner's Guide

Lee Maxwell

© 2016

TABLE OF CONTENT

Introduction

I want to thank you and congratulate you for downloading the book, *"SQL: The Ultimate Beginner's Guide"*.

This book contains proven steps and strategies on how to understand that This site is completely committed to SQL SERVER, a particular usage of a social database server from MICROSOFT.SQL server has been in the business for as far back as three decades and has made some amazing progress from SQL 1.0, SQL 7.0 through to SQL SERVER 2016. We likewise began uncovering Azure related stuff furthermore advertise inclining innovation BigData et cetera. Number of willful and automatic DBAs , designers taking a shot at SQL databases continue ticking each day and the fundamental expectation of this site is to help and teach each of those out in the field and new database experts beginning their wander with the SQL server.

SQL-ARTICLES host's number of good articles identified with different SQL server highlights and accommodating T-

SQL scripts. Aside from this, the perusers and clients can get some information about SQL server in our FORUMS segment. We might want to keep up this site as a SQL server learning base and a specialized data trade point. Come in, observe and soak yourself in the rain of SQL SERVER.

SQL Server CROSS APPLY and OUTER APPLY

Issue : SQL Server 2005 presented the APPLY administrator, which is especially similar to a join statement and which permits joining between two table expressions i.e. joining a left/external table expression with a privilege/internal table expression. The contrast amongst join and APPLY administrator gets to be distinctly clear when you have a table-esteemed expression on the correct side and you need this table-esteemed expression to be assessed for every line from the left table expression. In this tip I will exhibit what APPLY administrator is, the way it contrasts from consistent JOINs and what are few of its applications.

Arrangement :The APPLY administrator permits you to join two table expressions;

the correct table expression is handled each time for every line from the left table expression. As you may have speculated, the left table expression is assessed first and after that correct table expression is assessed against every line of the left table expression for conclusive outcome set. The last outcome set contains all the chose sections from the left table expression took after by every one of the segments of right table expression.

Thanks again for downloading this book, I hope you enjoy it!

Chapter 1

Welcome to SQL

This site is completely committed to SQL SERVER, a particular usage of a social database server from MICROSOFT.SQL server has been in the business for as far back as three decades and has made some amazing progress from SQL 1.0, SQL 7.0 through to SQL SERVER 2016. We likewise began uncovering Azure related stuff furthermore advertise inclining innovation BigData et cetera. Number of willful and automatic DBAs , designers taking a shot at SQL databases continue ticking each day and the fundamental expectation of this site is to help and teach each of those out in the field and new database experts beginning their wander with the SQL server.

SQL-ARTICLES host's number of good articles identified with different SQL server highlights and accommodating T-SQL scripts. Aside from this, the perusers and clients can get some information about SQL server in our FORUMS segment. We might want to keep up this site as a SQL server learning base and a specialized data trade point. Come in, observe and soak yourself in the rain of SQL SERVER.

SQL Server CROSS APPLY and OUTER APPLY

Issue

SQL Server 2005 presented the APPLY administrator, which is especially similar to a join statement and which permits joining between two table expressions i.e. joining a left/external table expression with a privilege/internal table expression. The contrast amongst join and APPLY administrator gets to be distinctly clear when you have a table-esteemed expression on the correct side and you need this table-esteemed expression to be assessed for every line from the left table expression. In this tip I will exhibit what APPLY administrator is, the way it contrasts from consistent JOINs and what are few of its applications.

Arrangement

The APPLY administrator permits you to join two table expressions; the correct table expression is handled each time for every line from the left table expression. As you may have speculated, the left table expression is assessed first and after that correct table expression is assessed against every line of the left table expression for conclusive outcome set. The last outcome set contains all the chose sections from the left table expression took after by every one of the segments of right table expression.

The APPLY administrator comes in two variations, the CROSS APPLY and the OUTER APPLY. The CROSS APPLY administrator returns just those lines from left table expression (in its last yield) on the off chance that it matches with right table expression. At the end of the day, the correct table expression returns lines for left table expression coordinate as it were. Though the OUTER APPLY administrator gives back every one of the columns from left table expression regardless of its match with the correct table expression. For those lines for which there are no relating matches in right table expression, it contains NULL values in sections of right table expression. So you may now finish up, the CROSS APPLY is semantically proportionate to INNER JOIN (or to be more exact its like a CROSS JOIN with a related sub-inquiry) with an understood join state of 1=1 though OUTER APPLY is semantically equal to LEFT OUTER JOIN.

You may think about whether the same can be accomplished with general JOIN proviso then why and when to utilize APPLY administrator? In spite of the fact that the same can be accomplished with typical JOIN, the need of APPLY emerges in the event that you have table-esteemed expression on right part furthermore at times utilization of APPLY administrator help the execution of your question. Give me a chance to clarify you with help of a few illustrations.

Script #1 makes a Department table to hold data about offices. At that point it makes an Employee table which hold data about the representatives. If it's not too much trouble take note of, every worker has a place with an office, consequently the Employee table has referential honesty with the Department table.

Script #1 - Creating some brief items to take a shot at...

Utilize [tempdb]

GO

On the off chance that EXISTS (SELECT * FROM sys.objects WHERE OBJECT_ID = OBJECT_ID(N'[Employee]') AND sort IN (N'U'))

Start

DROP TABLE [Employee]

END

GO

On the off chance that EXISTS (SELECT *
FROM sys.objects WHERE OBJECT_ID =
OBJECT_ID(N'[Department]') AND sort IN
(N'U'))

Start

DROP TABLE [Department]

END

Make TABLE [Department](

[DepartmentID]   [int]   NOT   NULL
PRIMARY KEY,

[Name] VARCHAR(250) NOT NULL,

) ON [PRIMARY]

Embed [Department] ([DepartmentID], [Name])

VALUES (1, N'Engineering')

Embed [Department] ([DepartmentID], [Name])

VALUES (2, N'Administration')

Embed [Department] ([DepartmentID], [Name])

VALUES (3, N'Sales')

Embed [Department] ([DepartmentID], [Name])

VALUES (4, N'Marketing')

Embed [Department] ([DepartmentID], [Name])

VALUES (5, N'Finance')

GO

Make TABLE [Employee](

[EmployeeID] [int] NOT NULL PRIMARY KEY,

[FirstName] VARCHAR(250) NOT NULL,

[LastName] VARCHAR(250) NOT NULL,

[DepartmentID]   [int]   NOT   NULL
REFERENCES
[Department](DepartmentID),

) ON [PRIMARY]

GO

Embed   [Employee]   ([EmployeeID],
[FirstName],   [LastName],
[DepartmentID])

VALUES (1, N'Orlando', N'Gee', 1)

Embed   [Employee]   ([EmployeeID],
[FirstName],   [LastName],
[DepartmentID])

VALUES (2, N'Keith', N'Harris', 2)

Embed   [Employee]   ([EmployeeID], [FirstName],   [LastName], [DepartmentID])

VALUES (3, N'Donna', N'Carreras', 3)

Embed   [Employee]   ([EmployeeID], [FirstName],   [LastName], [DepartmentID])

VALUES (4, N'Janet', N'Gates', 3)

In the first place question in Script #2 chooses information from Department table and uses CROSS APPLY to assess the Employee table for every record of the Department table. Second question essentially joins the Department table with the Employee table and all the coordinating records are delivered.

Script #2 - CROSS APPLY and INNER JOIN

```sql
SELECT * FROM Department D

CROSS APPLY

(

SELECT * FROM Employee E

WHERE         E.DepartmentID         =
D.DepartmentID

) A

GO

SELECT * FROM Department D

Internal   JOIN   Employee   E   ON
D.DepartmentID = E.DepartmentID
GO
```

In the event that you take a gander at the outcomes they delivered, it is precisely the same set; not just that even the execution get ready for these questions are like each other and has meet inquiry cost, as should be obvious in the picture beneath. So what is the utilization of APPLY administrator? How can it contrast from a JOIN and how can it help in composing more productive questions. I will examine this later, however first let me demonstrate to you a case of OUTER APPLY too.

The primary inquiry in Script #3 chooses information from Department table and uses OUTER APPLY to assess the Employee table for every record of the Department table. For those columns for which there is not a match in Employee table, those lines contains NULL values as should be obvious if there should arise an occurrence of line 5 and 6. The second inquiry essentially utilizes a LEFT OUTER JOIN between the Department table and the Employee table. Not surprisingly the question gives back all lines from Department table; notwithstanding for those columns for which there is no match in the Employee table.

Script #3 - OUTER APPLY and LEFT OUTER JOIN

```
SELECT * FROM Department D

External APPLY

(

SELECT * FROM Employee E

WHERE        E.DepartmentID        =
D.DepartmentID

) A
GO

SELECT * FROM Department D
```

LEFT OUTER JOIN Employee E ON
D.DepartmentID = E.DepartmentID

GO

Despite the fact that the over two inquiries give back a similar data, the execution plan is somewhat unique. In spite of the fact that cost insightful there is very little contrast, the inquiry with the OUTER APPLY utilizes a Compute Scalar administrator (which has an expected administrator cost of 0.0000103 or right around 0% of aggregate question cost) before Nested Loops administrator to assess and create the sections of Employee table.

Presently comes an ideal opportunity to see where the APPLY administrator is truly required. In Script #4, I am making a table-esteemed capacity which acknowledges DepartmentID as its parameter and returns every one of the representatives who have a place with this office. The following inquiry chooses information from Department table and uses CROSS APPLY to join with the capacity we made. It passes the DepartmentID for every line from the external table expression (for our situation Department table) and assesses the capacity for every line like an associated subquery. The following inquiry utilizes the OUTER APPLY as a part of place of CROSS APPLY and consequently not at all like CROSS APPLY which returned just related information, the OUTER APPLY returns non-connected information also, setting NULLs into the missing sections.

Script #4 - APPLY with table-esteemed capacity

In the event that EXISTS (SELECT * FROM sys.objects WHERE OBJECT_ID = OBJECT_ID(N'[fn_GetAllEmployeeOfADep artment]') AND sort IN (N'IF'))

Start

DROP   FUNCTION dbo.fn_GetAllEmployeeOfADepartment

```
END


GO


Make                    FUNCTION
dbo.fn_GetAllEmployeeOfADepartment(@
DeptID AS INT)


RETURNS TABLE


AS


RETURN


(


SELECT * FROM Employee E


WHERE E.DepartmentID = @DeptID
)
```

GO

SELECT * FROM Department D

CROSS   APPLY
dbo.fn_GetAllEmployeeOfADepartment(D.
DepartmentID)

GO

SELECT * FROM Department D

External   APPLY
dbo.fn_GetAllEmployeeOfADepartment(D.
DepartmentID)

GO

So now in the event that you are pondering, would we be able to utilize a straightforward participate set up of the above questions? At that point the answer is NO, in the event that you supplant CROSS/OUTER APPLY in the above questions with INNER JOIN/LEFT OUTER JOIN, determine ON condition (something as 1=1) and run the inquiry, you will get "The multi-part identifier "D.DepartmentID" couldn't be bound." mistake. This is on the grounds that with JOINs the execution setting of external inquiry is unique in relation to the execution setting of the capacity (or an inferred table), and you can not tie an esteem/variable from the external question to the capacity as a parameter. Consequently the APPLY administrator is required for such inquiries.

So in outline the APPLY administrator is required when you need to utilize table-esteemed capacity in the question, however it can likewise be utilized with an inline SELECT explanations.

Presently let me demonstrate to you another inquiry with a Dynamic Management Function (DMF). Script #5 gives back all the as of now executing client inquiries with the exception of the questions being executed by the present session. As should be obvious the script beneath, the sys.dm_exec_requests dynamic administration view is being CROSS APPLY'ed with the sys.dm_exec_sql_text dynamic administration work which acknowledges an "arrangement handle" for the *q*uestion and the same "arrangement handle" is being passed from the left/external expression to the capacity to work and to give back the information.

Script #5 - APPLY with Dynamic Management Function (DMF)

Utilize ace

GO

SELECT   DB_NAME(database_id)   AS [Database], [text] AS [Query]

FROM sys.dm_exec_requests r

CROSS APPLY
sys.dm_exec_sql_text(r.plan_handle) st

WHERE session_Id > 50 - Consider spids for clients just, no framework spids.

What's more, session_Id NOT IN (@@SPID) - Do exclude ask for from current spid.

It would be ideal if you take note of the [text] section in the above question gives back the all inquiries submitted in a clump; on the off chance that you need to see just dynamic (right now executing) inquiry you can utilize statement_start_offset and statement_end_offset segments to trim the dynamic part of the inquiry. Tim Ford has given a decent clarification of use of these sections in his How to separate the present running summons in SQL Server tip.

As I let you know before there are sure situations where an inquiry with APPLY administrator performs superior to anything a **q**uestion with standard joins yet I am not going to dig into much subtle elements rather here are a few articles which examine this theme in more prominent points of interest.

Chapter 2

INNER JOINS versus CROSS APPLY

• Using CROSS APPLY to streamline joins on BETWEEN conditions

If it's not too much trouble note, APPLY administrator is not an ANSI administrator but instead an expansion of SQL Server T-SQL (accessible in SQL Server 2005 or more), so in the event that you plan to port your database to some different DBMS take this into your contemplations.

Part Delimited Strings Using XML in SQL Server

Issue

This article will help designers searching for an approach to part delimited strings in a solitary inquiry utilizing XML. We for the most part utilize a client characterized capacity to do this, which you have likely found in many spots that parts the string in light of the delimiter passed. In any case, with regards to isolating the string in a solitary question with no assistance of a client characterized work there are very few choices. I have found a much easier and shorter method for part any string in view of a delimiter. I will utilize the force of XML to do the part of the string rather than a client characterized work.

Arrangement

Suppose for instance there is a string "A,B,C,D,E" and I need to part it in view of the delimiter ','.

The initial step is change over that string into XML and supplant the delimiter with some begin and end XML labels.

Pronounce @xml as xml,@str as varchar(100),@delimiter as varchar(10)

```
SET @str='A,B,C,D,E'


SET @delimiter =','


SET              @xml              =
cast(('<X>'+replace(@str,@delimiter
,'</X><X>')+'</X>') as xml)


SELECT @xml
```

Here is the thing that this looks like after the delimiter "," is supplanted by </X><X> labels. When you see the yield in the wake of changing over the string into XML, you will have the capacity to see the string as appeared in the picture underneath:

Once the string is changed over into XML you can without much of a stretch in*q*uiry that utilizing XQuery

Proclaim @xml as xml,@str as varchar(100),@delimiter as varchar(10)

SET @str='A,B,C,D,E'

SET @delimiter =','

SET @xml = cast(('<X>'+replace(@str,@delimiter ,'</X><X>')+'</X>') as xml)

SELECT N.value('.', 'varchar(10)') as esteem FROM @xml.nodes('X') as T(N)

.This will give the yield as an isolated string as:

Presently, say I have a table that has an ID segment and comma isolated string information as demonstrated as follows.

Proclaim @t TABLE(ID INT IDENTITY, information VARCHAR(50))

Embed INTO @t(data) SELECT
"AA,AB,AC,AD"

Embed INTO @t(data) SELECT
"BA,BB,BC"

SELECT * FROM @t

I can utilize the technique appeared above to part the string.

Pronounce @t TABLE(ID INT IDENTITY, information VARCHAR(50))

Embed INTO @t(data) SELECT
"AA,AB,AC,AD"

Embed INTO @t(data) SELECT
"BA,BB,BC"

SELECT F1.id,

```sql
F1.data,

O.splitdata

FROM

(

SELECT *,

cast('<X>'+replace(F.data,',','</X><X>')+'
</X>' as XML) as xmlfilter from @t F

)F1

CROSS APPLY

(
```

SELECT fdata.D.value('.','varchar(50)') as splitdata

FROM f1.xmlfilter.nodes('X') as fdata(D)) 0

At the point when the above is run this is the yield we get:

This is what is being finished. Above all else I cast the "information" section of table @t into a XML information sort by supplanting the delimiter with beginning and consummation labels '<X></X>'.

I have utilized 'CROSS APPLY' for part the information. The APPLY statement gives you a chance to join a table to a table-esteemed capacity. The APPLY provision acts like a JOIN without the ON condition and comes in two flavors: CROSS and OUTER.

• The OUTER APPLY provision returns every one of the columns on the left side (@t) whether they give back any lines in the table-esteemed capacity or not. The segments that the table-esteemed capacity returns are invalid if no lines are returned.

• The CROSS APPLY just returns columns from the left side (@t) if the table-esteemed capacity returns lines.

This tip ideally demonstrates to you the force of XML and the utilization of 'CROSS APPLY'. There are different alternatives to part strings in a solitary question utilizing recursive CTEs, however we will spare that for another tip.

Next Steps

• Now at whatever point part of string is required you can without much of a stretch cast the string into XML, by supplanting the delimiter with XML begin and end labels and afterward utilize the strategy appeared above to part the string.

• Take some an opportunity to get acquainted with the XML highlights in SQL Server to check whether you can rearrange your handling.

SQL Server Monitoring Scripts with the DMVs

Issue

As a SQL Server DBA, devoted to checking and regulating many occupied OLTP creation situations, I generally wind up attempting to answer questions like: What was SQL Server doing the previous evening when the end clients were encountering moderate application reaction times? Was the issue from SQL Server? On the other hand would it say it was a system or an application issue? The responses to such inquiries are never simple to distinguish. On the off chance that I just realized what SQL Server was doing at that particular point in time. On the off chance that I recognized what SQL Server was doing by then, it might help me comprehend if the issues was a SQL Server execution issue or not . So how might I make sense of this? On the off chance that you don't host a third get-together observing apparatus set up, the main path is to always screen SQL Server. To do this without being excessively meddling, we have to depend on the SQL Server DMVs.

Arrangement

This tip quickly depicts how to effectively consolidate the utilization of two SQL Server DMV's (sys.dm_exec_requests and sys.dm_exec_sessions) to make a simple, non meddlesome and extremely productive instrument to screen asks for that are being executed against a SQL Server 2005 or SQL Server 2008 occasion. The main two DMV's that I should make my T-SQL based screen script are sys.dm_exec_requests and sys.dm_exec_sessions. It is not my expectation to clarify the subtle elements of those two DMV's, I will just join them to show what great data originates from them.

The accompanying script proves to be useful on the grounds that it catches the code the SQL Server motor is preparing anytime. Here is that *q*uestion:

```
SELECT      T.[text],      P.[query_plan],
S.[program_name], S.[host_name],


S.[client_interface_name],  S.[login_name],
R.*


FROM sys.dm_exec_requests R


Inward JOIN sys.dm_exec_sessions S


ON S.session_id = R.session_id


CROSS                              APPLY
sys.dm_exec_sql_text(sql_handle) AS T
```

CROSS   APPLY
sys.dm_exec_query_plan(plan_handle)   As
P

GO

Keeping in mind the end goal to make our basic checking apparatus, how about we make the accompanying observing table. Here is the script:

Make TABLE [dbo].[MyMonitorTable](

[text] [nvarchar](max) NULL,

[query_plan] [xml] NULL,

[host_name] [nvarchar](128) NULL,

[program_name] [nvarchar](128) NULL,

[client_interface_name]   [nvarchar](32) NULL,

[login_name] [nvarchar](128) NOT NULL,

[session_id] [smallint] NOT NULL,

[request_id] [int] NOT NULL,

[start_time] [datetime] NOT NULL,

[status] [nvarchar](30) NOT NULL,

[command] [nvarchar](16) NOT NULL,

[sql_handle] [varbinary](64) NULL,

[statement_start_offset] [int] NULL,

[statement_end_offset] [int] NULL,

[plan_handle] [varbinary](64) NULL,

[database_id] [smallint] NOT NULL,

[user_id] [int] NOT NULL,

[connection_id] [uniqueidentifier] NULL,

[blocking_session_id] [smallint] NULL,

[wait_type] [nvarchar](60) NULL,

[wait_time] [int] NOT NULL,

[last_wait_type] [nvarchar](60) NOT NULL,

[wait_resource] [nvarchar](256) NOT
NULL,

[open_transaction_count] [int] NOT NULL,

[open_resultset_count] [int] NOT NULL,

[transaction_id] [bigint] NOT NULL,

[context_info] [varbinary](128) NULL,

[percent_complete] [real] NOT NULL,

[estimated_completion_time] [bigint] NOT
NULL,

[cpu_time] [int] NOT NULL,

[total_elapsed_time] [int] NOT NULL,

[scheduler_id] [int] NULL,

[task_address] [varbinary](8) NULL,

[reads] [bigint] NOT NULL,

[writes] [bigint] NOT NULL,

[logical_reads] [bigint] NOT NULL,

[text_size] [int] NOT NULL,

[language] [nvarchar](128) NULL,

[date_format] [nvarchar](3) NULL,

[date_first] [smallint] NOT NULL,

[quoted_identifier] [bit] NOT NULL,

```sql
[arithabort] [bit] NOT NULL,

[ansi_null_dflt_on] [bit] NOT NULL,

[ansi_defaults] [bit] NOT NULL,

[ansi_warnings] [bit] NOT NULL,

[ansi_padding] [bit] NOT NULL,

[ansi_nulls] [bit] NOT NULL,

[concat_null_yields_null] [bit] NOT NULL,

[transaction_isolation_level]    [smallint]
NOT NULL,

[lock_timeout] [int] NOT NULL,
```

[deadlock_priority] [int] NOT NULL,

[row_count] [bigint] NOT NULL,

[prev_error] [int] NOT NULL,

[nest_level] [int] NOT NULL,

[granted_query_memory] [int] NOT NULL,

[executing_managed_code] [bit] NOT NULL,

[group_id] [int] NOT NULL,

[query_hash] [binary](8) NULL,

[query_plan_hash] [binary](8) NULL

)

GO

To screen the SQL Server action in a computerized way, make a SQL Server Agent Job that executes the code underneath consistently.

Embed INTO MyMonitorTable

SELECT T.text, P.query_plan, S.host_name, S.program_name, S.client_interface_name, S.login_name, R.*

FROM sys.dm_exec_requests R

JOIN sys.dm_exec_sessions S on S.session_id=R.session_id

CROSS APPLY sys.dm_exec_sql_text(sql_handle) AS T

CROSS APPLY
sys.dm_exec_query_plan(plan_handle) As
P

GO

After the employment has been running
for a considerable length of time or days,
we can question the MyMonitorTable
table to see what SQL Server
proclamations have been caught, as
appeared in the picture beneath:

Script Caveats

Clarify that this straightforward checking
script does not catch all exchanges like
SQL Server Profiler does. This script with
the SQL Server Agent Job just specimens
SQL Server exchanges incrementally. You
won't catch all inquiries. This script is
gone for catching questions that are long
running, may bringing on blocking and
run much of the time.

Here are likewise a few segments to
concentrate on as you utilize the script:

- For preparatory investigating look at the accompanying segments:

o host_name

o program_name

o database_id

o user_id

o reads

o writes

o wait_type

o wait_time

o last_wait_type

o wait_resource

• The query_plan segment appears (in xml organize) the executed arrangement that a particular explanation utilized. A graphical arrangement representation is likewise accessible on the off chance that you tap on the XML arrange.

• The blocking_session_id indicates which session is at present hindering an announcement and the hold up sort.

• The statatement_text demonstrates what inquiry has been executed.

• Statement_start_offset and Statement_start_offset can be utilized to list the correct T-SQL explanation that was executed, inside the bunch work, at the particular point in time.

Next Steps

• Check out this script and run it in your improvement or QA situations to understand the outcomes and potential issues before they are elevated to your generation surroundings.

• Once you are alright with the script, consider utilizing it as a part of your creation surroundings to better comprehend your execution. Contingent upon your necessities you could execute the employment 24X7, amid ordinary business hours or similarly as required. You decide.

• Check out these related MSSQLTips:

o How to confine the present running orders in SQL Server

o Session State Settings for Cached SQL Server Query Plans

o Finding a SQL Server handle rate finish with element...

o Collecting Query Statistics for SQL Server 2005

o Identify last proclamation keep running for a particular SQL Server session.

Chapter 3

Gathering Query Statistics for SQL Server

Issue

With SQL Server 2005 DMVs, we can without much of a stretch discover inquiry execution insights. Each DBA has a most loved script to discover question execution details. I additionally have one. In any case, are every one of the questions caught by the DMVs? In this tip I will stroll through catching some of this information and show what is catch and what is not caught by the DMVs.

Arrangement

Here is a straightforward illustration which unmistakably demonstrates that not all question are caught in the DMVs.

This fantastic article was my beginning stage. I was running the example questions in that article and was interested to check whether they appeared in my inquiry details script, yet they didn't.

Here is my most loved script to discover inquiry details. This will demonstrate the quantity of times a question was executed, peruses, composes and the execution arrange.

The script gets information from these DMVs.

• dm_exec_query_stats

• dm_exec_sql_text

• dm_exec_query_plan

- Query Stats

```sql
SELECT

sdest.dbid

,sdest.[text] AS Batch_Object,

SUBSTRING(sdest.[text],
(sdeqs.statement_start_offset/2) + 1,

((CASE sdeqs.statement_end_offset

At the point when - 1 THEN
DATALENGTH(sdest.[text])        ELSE
sdeqs.statement_end_offset END

- sdeqs.statement_start_offset)/2) + 1) AS
SQL_Statement

, sdeqp.query_plan
```

```
, sdeqs.execution_count

, sdeqs.total_physical_reads

,(sdeqs.total_physical_reads/sdeqs.execut
ion_count) AS average_physical_reads

, sdeqs.total_logical_writes

,
(sdeqs.total_logical_writes/sdeqs.executi
on_count) AS average_logical_writes

, sdeqs.total_logical_reads

,
(sdeqs.total_logical_reads/sdeqs.executio
n_count) AS average_logical_lReads

, sdeqs.total_clr_time
```

```
,
(sdeqs.total_clr_time/sdeqs.execution_co
unt) AS average_CLRTime


, sdeqs.total_elapsed_time


,
(sdeqs.total_elapsed_time/sdeqs.executio
n_count) AS average_elapsed_time


, sdeqs.last_execution_time


, sdeqs.creation_time


FROM sys.dm_exec_query_stats AS sdeqs


CROSS                            apply
sys.dm_exec_sql_text(sdeqs.sql_handle)
AS sdest
```

CROSS apply sys.dm_exec_query_plan(sdeqs.plan_handle) AS sdeqp

WHERE sdeqs.last_execution_time > DATEADD(HH,- 2,GETDATE())

What's more, sdest.dbid = (SELECT DB_ID('AdventureWorks'))

Arrange BY execution_count DESC

For a perfect server, that has quite recently been begun or on the off chance that we run DBCC FREEPROCCACHE, if the above question is run we can see that no information is caught as demonstrated as follows.

We should see what is caught by the DMVs and what is not caught.

Execute Script-1 a couple times in inquiry analyzer and after that execute the Query Stats script above and check whether script-1 appears in the outcomes.

- Script-1

Utilize AdventureWorks

GO

Executive sp_executesql

@stmt = N'select * from Sales.SalesOrderDetail where ProductID = @ProductID',

@params = N'@ProductID int', @ProductID = 870

GO

As should be obvious beneath it doesn't appear.

In this way, we now know sp_executes*q*l in*q*uiries are not caught in the DMVs

Execute Script-2 few circumstances in question analyzer and afterward execute the Query Stats script above and check whether script-2 appears in the outcomes.

- Script-2

Utilize AdventureWorks

GO

SELECT * FROM Sales.SalesOrderDetail WHERE ProductID = 870

As should be obvious underneath it doesn't appear.

Along these lines, we now know standalone *q*uestions are not caught in the DMVs. This regards know since most designers are extremely open to composing inline T-SQL in their application code. Along these lines, those inline T-SQL articulations are not caught in the DMVs

Presently, how about we make a put away technique that has a select proclamation utilizing script-3 beneath. After the SP has been made, execute the put away proc dbo.DMVQueryTest a couple times in inquiry analyzer and afterward execute the Query Stats script to check whether the put away technique and select explanation appears in the outcomes.

- Script-3

Utilize AdventureWorks

GO

In the event that OBJECT_ID('dbo.DMVQueryTest') IS NOT NULL

DROP PROC dbo.DMVQueryTest

GO

Make PROC dbo.DMVQueryTest

@productId INT

AS

Start

SELECT * FROM Sales.SalesOrderDetail WHERE ProductID = @productId

RETURN 0

END

GO

Executive dbo.DMVQueryTest 870

As should be obvious underneath we can now observe this in the in*q*uiry details.

In this way, SQL articulations that are inside a put away methodology are caught in the DMVs. This demonstrates NOT all T-SQL executed against a database is caught in the DMVs. This is another motivation behind why put away methodology are the best strategy for information related operations, so we can track their execution and utilization utilizing DMVs.

Things being what they are the issue is with attempting to incorporate the execution arrange. On the off chance that we run the accompanying script we can see the information, yet we don't get the execution gets ready for the greater part of the SQL clumps that are run.

SELECT TOP 5 creation_time, last_execution_time, total_clr_time,

total_clr_time/execution_count AS [Avg CLR Time], last_clr_time,

execution_count,

SUBSTRING(st.TEXT, (*q*s.statement_start_offset/2) + 1,

((CASE statement_end_offset

At the point when - 1 THEN DATALENGTH(st.TEXT)

```sql
ELSE qs.statement_end_offset END


 - qs.statement_start_offset)/2) + 1) AS statement_text


FROM sys.dm_exec_query_stats AS qs


CROSS                               APPLY
sys.dm_exec_sql_text(qs.sql_handle) AS st


Arrange                                    BY
total_clr_time/execution_count DESC;


GO
```

Chapter 4

Here is the outcome.

Note: Upon further examination of this inquiry in light of contribution from yuewah, the issue is with the line of code that is remarked out underneath that was restricting the information to questions with a database id for AdventureWorks. In the event that this line is remarked out the script will give back the outcomes for the questions. The purpose behind this is the dbid section is NULL for specially appointed and arranged SQL articulations, so attempting to constrain ths to just questions from the AdventureWorks database expelled these inquiries from the resultset.

- Query Stats

SELECT

sdest.dbid

,sdest.[text] AS Batch_Object,

SUBSTRING(sdest.[text],
(sde*q*s.statement_start_offset/2) + 1,

((CASE sdeqs.statement_end_offset

At the point when - 1 THEN
DATALENGTH(sdest.[text]) ELSE
sde*q*s.statement_end_offset END

- sde*q*s.statement_start_offset)/2) + 1) AS
SQL_Statement

, sdeqp.query_plan

, sde*q*s.execution_count

, sdeqs.total_physical_reads

,(sdeqs.total_physical_reads/sdeqs.execut
ion_count) AS average_physical_reads

, sdeqs.total_logical_writes

,
(sdeqs.total_logical_writes/sdeqs.executi
on_count) AS average_logical_writes

, sdeqs.total_logical_reads

,
(sdeqs.total_logical_reads/sdeqs.executio
n_count) AS average_logical_lReads

, sdeqs.total_clr_time

,
(sdeqs.total_clr_time/sdeqs.execution_co
unt) AS average_CLRTime

, sdeqs.total_elapsed_time

,
(sde*q*s.total_elapsed_time/sde*q*s.executio
n_count) AS average_elapsed_time

, sde*q*s.last_execution_time

, sdeqs.creation_time

FROM sys.dm_exec_query_stats AS sde*q*s

CROSS apply
sys.dm_exec_s*q*l_text(sde*q*s.s*q*l_handle)
AS sdest

CROSS apply
sys.dm_exec_query_plan(sdeqs.plan_hand
le) AS sde*q*p

WHERE sde*q*s.last_execution_time >
DATEADD(HH,- 2,GETDATE())

- AND sdest.dbid = (SELECT DB_ID('AdventureWorks'))

Arrange BY execution_count DESC

Next Steps

• Keep this as a top priority when you are utilizing the DMVs for inquiry use and execution details. On the off chance that you are utilizing inline T-SQL and sp_executesql you may not catch the greater part of the information that you require.

• Also, consider utilizing put away methodology for all information related operations as opposed to utilizing inline T-SQL or sp_executesql in your application code.

• Also, set aside the opportunity to peruse Books Online to comprehend when certain **q**ualities are accessible and when they are not accessible.

The most effective method to Find Keywords in SQL Server Stored Procs and Functions

Issue

How often have you needed to investigate or roll out improvements to a current database that is not archived legitimately or totally? Indeed, even need to search for a particular put away methodology that references a particular table or process? On the off chance that you have suggest information of the database then this may not be **q**uite a bit of an issue for you. What happens if this database is from an outer engineer, a turn-key arrangement supplier, or created by another person inside your organization? In the event that you use the INFORMATION_SCHEMA.ROUTINES view to look into and investigate this issue, the errand goes from overwhelming to a cake-walk.

Arrangement

The INFORMATION_SCHEMA.ROUTINES see, presented in SQL 2000 uncovered metadata in the present database in accordance with substance got from the syscomments and sysobjects framework sees (2005) and framework tables (2000). It contains one line for every capacity and put away method in the database for which the present client has rights. This is an imperative note to make. In the event that you have restricted rights to the database, INFORMATION_SCHEMA.ROUTINES may not give back an entire arrangement of results in accordance with the question you are executing.

On the off chance that you are hunting down a particular watchword or square of content you can just question the INFORMATION_SCHEMA.ROUTINES see as takes after, substituting your look string for "Catchphrase":

SELECT ROUTINE_NAME,
ROUTINE_DEFINITION

FROM
INFORMATION_SCHEMA.ROUTINES

WHERE ROUTINE_DEFINITION LIKE
"%KEYWORD%"

What's more,
ROUTINE_TYPE='PROCEDURE'

Arrange BY ROUTINE_NAME

This is what might as well be called
running the accompanying question
specifically against the framework
tables/sees:

SELECT sys.sysobjects.name,
sys.syscomments.text

FROM sys.sysobjects INNER JOIN syscomments

ON sys.sysobjects.id = sys.syscomments.id

WHERE sys.syscomments.text LIKE "%KEYWORD%"

What's more, sys.sysobjects.type = "P"

Arrange BY sys.sysobjects.NAME

The INFORMATION_SCHEMA.ROUTINES view can be utilized to scan for substance of capacities too. Essentially modify your WHERE provision as takes after, substituting your hunt string set up of "Catchphrase" at the end of the day:

SELECT ROUTINE_NAME, ROUTINE_DEFINITION

FROM
INFORMATION_SCHEMA.ROUTINES

WHERE ROUTINE_DEFINITION LIKE
"%KEYWORD%"

Also, ROUTINE_TYPE='FUNCTION'

Arrange BY ROUTINE_NAME

To highlight the way that this procedure
is in reverse good to Microsoft SQL Server
2000, I've run the accompanying inquiry
against the Northwind database. I'm keen
on discovering all the put away strategies
that use the ROUND() capacity:

Utilize Northwind

GO

SELECT ROUTINE_NAME,
ROUTINE_DEFINITION

FROM
INFORMATION_SCHEMA.ROUTINES

WHERE ROUTINE_DEFINITION LIKE
"%ROUND%"

What's more,
ROUTINE_TYPE='PROCEDURE'

Arrange BY ROUTINE_NAME

GO

From this I am ready to establish that
there are two put away methods using
that capacity.

New DMF for SQL Server 2008
sys.dm_fts_parser to parse a string

Issue

Ordinarily we need to part a string into a cluster and get a rundown of every word independently. The sys.dm_fts_parser capacity will help us in these cases. More over, this capacity will likewise separate the commotion words and correct match words. The sys.dm_fts_parser can be likewise effective for troubleshooting purposes. It can help you check how the word breaker and stemmer functions for a given contribution for Full Text Search.

Arrangement

In SQL 2008 and forward, with Integrated Full Text Search (iFTS) we can now effectively part words in a variety of strings with the assistance of the dynamic administration work sys.dm_fts_parser. This capacity takes a full content question and splits it up utilizing the word breaker rules, applies stop records and any arranged thesaurus.

Authorization Required

This requires participation of the sysadmin settled server part and get to rights to the predetermined stoplist.

Sentence structure

sys.dm_fts_parser('query_string', lcid, stoplist_id, accent_sensitivity)

Parameter Description

query_string Query string that you need to parse. Question string can incorporate legitimate operators,inflectional structures and thesaurus.

lcid Locale identifier (LCID) of the word breaker

stoplist_id stoplist_id acknowledges the Int esteem as it were. stoplist_id is utilized by the word breaker distinguished by lcid. In the event that we indicate NULL not stoplist will be utilized. On the off chance that we determine 0 than the framework STOPLIST will be utilized.

Stop List will be remarkable in the database, you can recover the full content record stop list utilizing beneath question.

SELECT object_name(object_id), stoplist_id FROM sys.fulltext_indexes

accent_sensitivity Accepts the Boolean esteem just, 0 is for Insensitive and 1 is for touchy.

Cases

FORMSOF(THESAURUS, query_string)

You can check how the thesaurus extends or replaces all or part of the information utilizing the beneath question

```
SELECT * FROM sys.dm_fts_parser
('FORMSOF( THESAURUS,
"Administration Studio")', 2057, 0, 0)
```

Yield

FORMSOF(INFLECTIONAL, query_string)

To check how the word breaker and the stemmer parse an inquiry term and its stemming frames, you can execute the beneath question.

```
SELECT * FROM sys.dm_fts_parser
('FORMSOF( INFLECTIONAL, "Working
System")', 2057, 0, 0)
```

Yield

sys.dm_fts_parser('query_string', lcid, stoplist_id, accent_sensitivity)

This question will part the words in a string.

SELECT * FROM sys.dm_fts_parser ('SQL or MySQL or Oracle or DB or innovations or the or dbservers', 1033, 0, 0)

Yield

Next Steps

• Use the unique character in the inquiry string and test the yield

• Use this capacity with a table utilizing a Cross Apply join.

Decide SQL Server memory use by database and protest

Issue

For some individuals, the way that SQL Server utilizes memory can be a touch of a mystery. A substantial rate of the memory your SQL Server occurrence uses is devoured by support pool (basically, information). Without a considerable measure of burrowing, it can be difficult to tell which of your databases expend the most cushion pool memory, and much more in this way, which protests inside those databases. This data can be very helpful, for instance, on the off chance that you are thinking about an application change to part your database over different servers, or attempting to distinguish databases that are possibility for union.

Arrangement

A Dynamic Management View (DMV) presented in SQL Server 2005, called sys.dm_os_buffer_descriptors, contains a column for each page that has been reserved in the cradle pool. Utilizing this DMV, you can rapidly figure out which database(s) are using the greater part of your cradle pool memory. When you have distinguished the databases that are involving a great part of the cradle pool, you can bore into them independently. In the accompanying *q*uestion, I first discover precisely how huge the cushion pool at present is (from the DMV sys.dm_os_performance_counters), permitting me to ascertain the rate of the cradle pool being utilized by every database:

- Note: *q*uestioning sys.dm_os_buffer_descriptors

- re*q*uires the VIEW_SERVER_STATE authorization.

Announce @total_buffer INT;

SELECT @total_buffer = cntr_value

```
FROM sys.dm_os_performance_counters

WHERE RTRIM([object_name]) LIKE
'%Buffer Manager'

Also, counter_name = 'Database Pages';

;WITH src AS

(

SELECT

database_id, db_buffer_pages =
COUNT_BIG(*)

FROM sys.dm_os_buffer_descriptors

- WHERE database_id BETWEEN 5 AND
32766
```

Gather BY database_id

)

SELECT

[db_name] = CASE [database_id] WHEN 32767

At that point 'Asset DB'

ELSE DB_NAME([database_id]) END,

db_buffer_pages,

db_buffer_MB = db_buffer_pages/128,

db_buffer_percent = CONVERT(DECIMAL(6,3),

db_buffer_pages * 100.0/@total_buffer)

FROM src

Arrange BY db_buffer_MB DESC;

In the above question, I've incorporated
the framework databases, however you
can prohibit them by uncommenting the
WHERE condition inside the CTE. Take
note of that the real channel may need to
change with future forms of SQL Server;
for instance, in SQL Server 2012, there is
another database for Integration Services
called SSISDB. You might need to watch
out for framework databases just to have
an entire picture, seeing as there isn't
much you can do about their cradle pool
use in any case - unless you are utilizing
expert or msdb for your own particular
custom articles.

That all said, here are halfway outcomes
from an example on my neighborhood
virtual machine:

Unmistakably, the SQLSentry database - while just speaking to 258 MB - involves around 70% of my support pool for this example. So now I realize that I can bore into that database particularly on the off chance that I need to find the articles that are taking up the majority of that memory. You can by and by utilize the sys.dm_os_buffer_descriptors just this time, rather than conglomerating the page tallies at the database level, we can use an arrangement of list perspectives to decide the quantity of pages (and thusly measure of memory) committed to every question.

Utilize SQLSentry;

GO

;WITH src AS

(

SELECT

[Object] = o.name,

[Type] = o.type_desc,

[Index] = COALESCE(i.name, ''),

[Index_Type] = i.type_desc,

p.[object_id],

p.index_id,

au.allocation_unit_id

FROM

sys.partitions AS p

Inward JOIN

sys.allocation_units AS au

ON p.hobt_id = au.container_id

Inward JOIN

sys.objects AS o

ON p.[object_id] = o.[object_id]

Inward JOIN

sys.indexes AS i

ON o.[object_id] = i.[object_id]

Furthermore, p.index_id = i.index_id

WHERE

au.[type] IN (1,2,3)

Furthermore, o.is_ms_shipped = 0

)

SELECT

src.[Object],

src.[Type],

src.[Index],

src.Index_Type,

buffer_pages = COUNT_BIG(b.page_id),

buffer_mb = COUNT_BIG(b.page_id)/128

FROM

src

Inward JOIN

sys.dm_os_buffer_descriptors AS b

ON src.allocation_unit_id =
b.allocation_unit_id

WHERE

b.database_id = DB_ID()

Amass BY

src.[Object],

src.[Type],

src.[Index],

src.Index_Type

Arrange BY

buffer_pages DESC;

Here are the outcomes from this
database. See that I've caught both
grouped and non-bunched files, for
bunched tables and piles, and for
illustrative purposes I have additionally
made an ordered view.

It would be ideal if you remember that the
support pool is in steady flux, and that
this last question has expressly sifted
through framework objects, so the
numbers won't generally include
pleasantly. Still, this ought to give you a

genuinely smart thought of which items are utilizing your support pool the most.

At the point when examining the execution of your servers, cushion pool information is just a part of the photo, however it's one that is frequently ignored. Counting this information will help you to settle on better and more educated choices about bearing and scale.

Next Steps

• Take a stock of the most astounding cradle pool customers on your servers, and check whether the outcomes amaze you.

• Make an arrangement to intermittently survey this data and look for critical changes.

• Review the accompanying tips and different assets:

Finding a SQL Server handle rate finish with DMVs

Issue

A few assignments that are keep running in SQL Sever set aside a long opportunity to run and it is once in a while hard to tell whether these errands are advancing or not. One normal method for discovering that status is to take a gander at the information came back from sp_who2 or sp_lock to guarantee that things are as yet working and the procedure is not hung. With SQL Server 2005 a few element administration sees have been included, so we should investigate some of these and how they can help.

Arrangement

As said above utilizing sp_who2 or utilizing the GUI instruments you can get a thought of what is running and the present status of these errands. With SQL

Server 2005 a few element administration sees have been included and we will investigate two of these so you can increase some extra knowledge into your preparing.

The two DMVs that we will take a gander at are:

- dm_exec_requests

- dm_exec_sessions

Information can be chosen from these DMVs specifically utilizing a SELECT proclamation.

How about we investigate running a DBCC CHECKDB which regularly sets aside a great deal of opportunity to process and see what data we get once more from sp_who2 and additionally these new DMVs. We will run this against the AdventureWorks database.

To do this we open another inquiry window and after that run the accompanying:

utilize AdventureWorks

GO

DBCC CHECKDB

At the point when taking a gander at the DMVs and the yield from sp_who2 we get the outcomes recorded beneath. When I ran this my session_id was 68, so you should utilize the session_id that is being utilized to run the DBCC charge. This can be found on the base left of the question window.

SELECT * FROM sys.dm_exec_sessions
WHERE session_id = 68

session_id 68

login_time 9/26/2007 9:16:49 AM

host_name EDGEWOOD-NB3

program_name Microsoft SQL Server
Management Studio - Query

host_process_id 1516

client_version 5

client_interface_name .Net SqlClient Data
Provider

security_id
0x0105000000000000515000000F094C8
5F782E9D1307E53B2BEB030000

login_name EDGEWOOD-NB3\DBA

nt_domain EDGEWOOD-NB3

nt_user_name DBA

status running

context_info 0x

cpu_time 68986

memory_usage 2

total_scheduled_time 169019

total_elapsed_time 214482

endpoint_id 2

last_request_start_time 9/26/2007 10:14:56 AM

last_request_end_time 9/26/2007
10:14:46 AM

reads 13870

writes 278

logical_reads 367884

is_user_process 1

text_size 2147483647

language us_english

date_format mdy

date_first 7

quoted_identifier 1

arithabort 1

ansi_null_dflt_on 1

ansi_defaults 0

ansi_warnings 1

ansi_padding 1

ansi_nulls 1

concat_null_yields_null 1

transaction_isolation_level 2

lock_timeout -1

deadlock_priority 0

row_count 248

prev_error 0

original_security_id
0x0105000000000000515000000F094C8
5F782E9D1307E53B2BEB030000

original_login_name EDGEWOOD-
NB3\DBA

last_successful_logon NULL

last_unsuccessful_logon NULL

unsuccessful_logons NULL

SELECT * FROM sys.dm_exec_requests
WHERE session_id = 68

session_id 68

request_id 00:00.0

start_time 14:55.5

status suspended

command DBCC TABLE CHECK

sql_handle
0x020000002E9F9D2A305AB0BB39774
2F3F884C999A41E7826

statement_start_offset 0

statement_end_offset -1

plan_handle
0x06000C002E9F9D2AB881CA05000000
000000000000000000

database_id 12

user_id 1

connection_id 16A82EE3-CB5F-4977-
AF2A-304E5DCB49E1

blocking_session_id 0

wait_type CXPACKET

wait_time 4125

last_wait_type CXPACKET

wait_resource

open_transaction_count 1

open_resultset_count 00:00.0

transaction_id 00:00.0

context_info 0x

percent_complete 84.66557

estimated_completion_time 1318

cpu_time 3829

total_elapsed_time 19627

scheduler_id 1

task_address 0x00989018

reads 1532

writes 5

logical_reads 30948

text_size 2147483647

language us_english

date_format mdy

date_first 7

quoted_identifier 1

arithabort 1

ansi_null_dflt_on 1

ansi_defaults 0

ansi_warnings 1

ansi_padding 1

ansi_nulls 1

concat_null_yields_null 1

transaction_isolation_level 2

lock_timeout -1

deadlock_priority 0

row_count 248

prev_error 0

nest_level 1

granted_*q*uery_memory 2140

executing_managed_code 0

sp_who2 68

SPID 68 68 68 68 68

Status SUSPENDED RUNNABLE
SUSPENDED

Login EDGEWOOD-NB3\DBA

HostName EDGEWOOD-NB3
EDGEWOOD-NB3 EDGEWOOD-NB3
EDGEWOOD-NB3 EDGEWOOD-NB3

BlkBy . .

DBName AdventureWorks
AdventureWorks AdventureWorks
AdventureWorks AdventureWorks

Command DBCC TABLE CHECK DBCC
TABLE CHECK DBCC TABLE CHECK DBCC
TABLE CHECK DBCC TABLE CHECK

CPUTime 72815 16 47 2359 2171

DiskIO 15685 0 0 578 648

LastBatch 9/26/2007 10:14 9/26/2007
10:14 9/26/2007 10:14 9/26/2007
10:14 9/26/2007 10:14

ProgramName Microsoft SQL Server
Management Studio - Query Microsoft
SQL Server Management Studio - Query
Microsoft SQL Server Management Studio
- Query Microsoft SQL Server
Management Studio - Query Microsoft
SQL Server Management Studio - Query

SPID 68 68 68 68 68

REQUESTID 0 0 0 0 0

From the above yield we can understand
the distinctive things that are happening.
The information from sp_who2 is useful,
yet it is extremely restricted. The one
thing we can see is that the DBCC has
generated different strings to run the
charge, yet not significantly more.

One thing to note from the
sys.dm_exec_requests is the
percent_complete segment (this is
highlighted previously). This gives you a
thought where things are and additionally
a thought that things are advancing the
length of this esteem keeps on expanding.

Next Steps

• As you can see these two DMVs give you
considerably more understanding then

sp_who2 gives you. So next time you are checking SQL Server 2005, bear in mind that these DMVs exist.

Chapter 5

Helpful administration data from SQL Server DMV

Issue

I'm beginning to get intrigued with the Dynamic Management Views in Microsoft SQL Server. What sort of data would I be able to gather from the sys.dm_os_sys_info DMV?

Arrangement

That DMV is an incredible hopping off point, since we'll have the capacity to take a gander at a couple of various uses for the sections uncovered in that view furthermore take a gander at how the DMVs have the likelihood of changing as new arrivals of SQL Server happen. Before making a plunge SQL Server 2005 and SQL Server 2008. To make sure you're mindful that these items change and advance after some time.

SQL Server 2005 Schema

SQL Server 2008 Schema

As you may see, there was a blueprint change from SQL Server 2005 to SQL Server 2008. The main, cpu_ticks_in_ms was wiped out after SQL Server 2005. Likewise, sqlserver_start_time_ms_ticks and sqlserver_start_time were included the arrival of SQL Server 2008 (setting aside a few minutes for the SQL benefits far simpler than in SQL Server 2005.) The cpu_ticks_in_ms was wiped out by Microsoft over worries that it was not figuring precisely. This figure can in any case be gotten by utilization of the accompanying capacity and works in both SQL Server 2005 and later:

[cpu_ticks]/[ms_ticks]

The expansion of sql_server_start_time in SQL Server 2008 takes into consideration the rearrangements in a question that takes into account the examination amongst server, and SQL begin times in one of the inquiries I'll be introducing later in this tip. Talking about scripts. It's a great opportunity to see what addresses this Dynamic Management View answers for us.

CPU - Based Information

What are the quantity of physical CPUs and center (otherwise known as virtual CPU) mean the server the SQL case is facilitated on?

```
SELECT cpu_count AS virtual_cpu_count,

cpu_count/hyperthread_ratio AS physical_cpu_count

FROM sys.[dm_os_sys_info];
```

What does the present CPU usage resemble?

Robert Pearl, in a 2009 article on SQL Server Central had given an inquiry that answers this particular question while inspecting the diagram changes in sys.dm_sys_info between SQL Server 2005 and 2008. My question is so like his that I didn't feel good giving it in this article without raising the apparition of written falsification. Rather I'll direct you toward his answer here and request that you look at his article as it goes past this question. The following is the thing that the yield of his question looks like against my test server:

Actually I am not an enthusiast of returning more data than is essential, so I would advocate not giving back the record_id. What I like about this question is that a DBA can pull this data effectively, without the need of remoting into the server and pulling up the Task Manager.

Shouldn't something be said about laborers, schedulers on the occasion?

At the point when a client interfaces with SQL through some application or program they will in the end present a charge to SQL Server to accomplish something. This "something" might be to make a table, embed a record, or select a scope of records from a table or set of tables. This "something" has a name: a Batch. The database motor will allocate the cluster to a session and may, if helpful for the operation of satisfying the group's command, split the clump up into at least one errands that will be relegated to a laborer (string) to keep running on a SQL scheduler. The quantity of specialists is controlled by the laborer pool, the extent of which is controlled by SQL Server by means of the maximum laborer strings setting. At the point when set to 0 the number of specialists is overseen by SQL Server and is based upon whether the occasion is running on a 32 or 64-bit stage furthermore on the check of CPUs. There is a table connected with these settled values in Books Online accessible from Microsoft. We can acquire a knowledge into the settings for max laborer check by questioning sys.dm_os_sys_info and contrasting it with that outline on Books Online.

The accompanying **q**uestion and two outcome sets were gotten from two indistinguishable cases running on the same SQL 2005 Enterprise Edition 64 bit bunch in my surroundings. You'll see that however the servers are indistinguishable, there are contrasts in their max_workers_count and aggregate scheduler check. This is on account of the setting for the primary occurrence appeared beneath was left at max specialists number = 0 while the second example had its setting for max laborers tally at 128.

SELECT

cpu_count ,

[max_workers_count],

[scheduler_count],

[scheduler_total_count]

FROM sys.[dm_os_sys_info] dosi

The qualities for scheduler_count and scheduler_total_count are connected with those schedulers ready to administration client strings for the case, and aggregate schedulers for all SQL Server strings including those not available to client strings.

Uptime Information

At the point when was the server last restarted?

SELECT

[ms_ticks] AS ms_since_restart,

```
[ms_ticks]/1000 AS
seconds_since_restart,


CAST([ms_ticks]/1000/60.0 AS
DECIMAL(15,2)) AS
minutes_since_restart,


CAST([ms_ticks]/1000/60/60.0 AS
DECIMAL(15,2)) AS hours_since_restart,


CAST([ms_ticks]/1000/60/60/24.0 AS
DECIMAL(15,2)) AS days_since_restart,


DATEADD(s,((-
1)*([ms_ticks]/1000)),GETDATE()) AS
time_of_last_restart


FROM sys.[dm_os_sys_info];
```

How does the server restart time contrast
with the SQL Server benefit begin time?
(SQL 2005 and later)

We can break down the distinction amongst server and SQL Server benefit begin time by taking a gander at when the make date of tempdb when contrasted with the data put away in sys.dm_os_sys_info. Be that as it may, as I displayed as of late on my blog, you can't depend on the create_date being precise in sys.databases when Daylight Savings Time is a variable. Just the sqlserver_start_time section in sys.dm_os_sys_info gives an exact bookkeeping to the administration begin time when the switch between Daylight Standard and Daylight Savings Time happens between the season of administration restart and the ebb and flow date. Sadly that segment does not exist until SQL Server 2008. You'll additionally see that there are slight contrasts between how the administration begin time is displayed between alternatives. I discovered this intriguing, yet couldn't locate a nice clarification in any of my examination.

SELECT

```
DATEADD(s,((-
1)*(DOSI.[ms_ticks]/1000)),GETDATE())
AS last_SERVER_restart,


D.create_date,


(DATEDIFF(s, DATEADD(s,((-
1)*(DOSI.[ms_ticks]/1000)),GETDATE()),
D.create_date)) AS recovery_time_seconds


FROM sys.[dm_os_sys_info] DOSI


CROSS JOIN sys.[databases] D


WHERE D.[name] = 'tempdb';


SELECT


DATEADD(s,((-
1)*(DOSI.[ms_ticks]/1000)),GETDATE())
AS last_SERVER_restart,
```

DOSI.s*q*lserver_start_time,

(DATEDIFF(s, DATEADD(s,((-1)*(DOSI.[ms_ticks]/1000)),GETDATE()), DOSI.s*q*lserver_start_time)) AS recovery_time_seconds

FROM sys.[dm_os_sys_info] DOSI;

Memory Based Information

Decide when AWE is being utilized on a SQL occurrence

SQL Server can use Address Windowing Extensions to dispense extra RAM where it is hamstrung by release restrictions for use in the cushion reserve. How this presents itself in sys.dm_os_sys_info is through the virtual_memory_in_bytes and bpool_visible segments. Underneath I introduce two screen shots of a similar in*q*uiry. The in*q*uiry was keep running against a SQL 2005 Enterprise 64-bit

example and afterward against a SQL
2008 Standard Edition 32-bit occasion:

SELECT

[physical_memory_in_bytes]/1024/1024
AS [physical_memory_mb],

[virtual_memory_in_bytes]/1024/1024
AS [virtual_memory_in_mb],

[bpool_committed]*8/1024 AS
[bpool_committed_mb],

[bpool_commit_target]*8/1024 AS
[bpool_commit_targt_mb],

[bpool_visible]*8/1024 AS
[bpool_visible_mb]

FROM sys.[dm_os_sys_info] dosi;

Example running with AWE

The main case (not running with AWE empowered) is a 64 bit introduce of SQL Server Enterprise Edition. It has 32,766 mb of physical memory, with the Maximum Server Memory (in MB) esteem set to 28,672 mb. As should be obvious, the conferred physical RAM in the cushion pool (bpool_committed), the required physical RAM in the cradle pool (bpool_commit_target), and the aggregate size of all supports in the cushion pool that can be specifically tended to are each of the 28,672 mb. This all focuses to the occurrence NOT utilizing AWE to address memory.

The second occurrence (running with AWE empowered) has 16,373 mb of physical RAM. For this situation, the bpool_committed_mb is equivalent to my settings for Maximum Server Memory (in MB) of 13,312 mb, however it needs to accomodate that setting by utilization of Address Windowing Extension to meet that objective. You'll see that the unmistakable measure of cradle pool

RAM is altogether littler than submitted or target cushion pool. This is an indication that AWE is empowered and it speaks to the extent of the mapping window utilized by means of AWE to get to physical memory for the support pool. For this situation that esteem is 1,416 mb. This is the measure of memory that can be utilized by the arrangement reserve, support pool, inquiry streamlining agent, and question motor without the need to page out or utilize AWE. At the point when completing this tip I was examining a superior strategy for finding when AWE is being utilized and kept running over an intriguing post by Slava Oks (blog). There is some hybrid in what was talked about here, yet it is a commendable read and I will just point you towards his thought on deciding when AWE is being utilized, so as not to deny him the page hit on his blog.

In general, this DMV gives you data identified with CPU, uptime, and memory settings on your SQL Server occurrence.

Making IO execution previews to discover SQL Server execution issues

Issue

I/O is a standout amongst the most tedious exercises in SQL Server. In the event that you can diminish the I/O hold up time then you can enhance execution. This should be possible with ordering and tuning inquiries, yet I/O issues may likewise be at the document level. In this tip we take a gander at how to distinguish particular documents that devour the most I/O movement utilizing a SQL Server DMV and making depictions for investigation.

Arrangement

The arrangement I recommend here is to gather I/O insights for a specific era and afterward contrast the information previews with recognize potential I/O bottlenecks. To begin with we will gather a gauge and after that once per day (or hour or at whatever time period) gather the insights again and check the distinction between two unique depictions.

The I/O measurements will be gathered from an inquiry utilizing sys.dm_io_virtual_file_stats and sys.master_files. The information that will be incorporated comprises of the accompanying information segments (Table from BOL).

Column Type Description

num_of_reads bigint Number of peruses issued on the document.

num_of_bytes_read bigint Total number of bytes read on this document.

io_stall_read_ms bigint Total time, in milliseconds, that the clients sat tight for peruses issued on the document.

num_of_writes bigint Number of composes made on this document.

num_of_bytes_written bigint Total number of bytes kept in touch with the document.

io_stall_write_ms bigint Total time, in milliseconds, that clients sat tight for composes to be finished on the document.

io_stall bigint Total time, in milliseconds, that clients sat tight for I/O to be finished on the document.

size_on_disk_bytes bigint Number of bytes utilized on the plate for this document. For meager documents, this number is the genuine number of bytes on the circle that are utilized for database depictions.

I/O Statistics gathering process

To begin with we should make tables to store the I/O measurements. The accompanying code will make two tables. You can place this in the ace database or whatever database you favor.

- make a table for preview grouping era

Make TABLE io_snapshots

(snap_id INT IDENTITY NOT NULL,

snapshot_creation_date DATETIME NOT NULL)

GO

Change TABLE io_snapshots ADD CONSTRAINT PK_io_snapshots PRIMARY KEY (snap_id)

GO

- make a table for the io measurements

Make TABLE io_snapshots_statistics

(snap_id INT NOT NULL,

[db_id] smallint NOT NULL,

[file_id] smallint NOT NULL,

database_name SYSNAME,

physical_file_name SYSNAME,

Diff_Number_of_reads bigint,

Diff_Bytes_Read bigint,

Diff_Read_stall_time_ms bigint,

Diff_Number_of_writes bigint,

Diff_Bytes_written bigint,

Diff_Write_stall_time_ms bigint,

Diff_Read_Write_stall_ms bigint,

size_on_disk_MB bigint)

GO

Change TABLE io_snapshots_statistics
ADD CONSTRAINT
PK_io_snapshots_statistics

Essential KEY (snap_id,[db_id], [file_id])

GO

Change TABLE io_snapshots_statistics
ADD CONSTRAINT
FK_io_snapshots_statistics_io_snapshots

Remote KEY (snap_id) REFERENCES
io_snapshots (snap_id)

GO

Second we should make the
accompanying two put away methods.

The primary SP (usp_io_vf_stats_snap)
embeds another I/O depiction of insights
every time it is run.

- The First Procedure.

Make PROC [dbo].[usp_io_vf_stats_snap]

AS

Start

SET NOCOUNT ON

Embed INTO io_snapshots (
snapshot_creation_date) SELECT
GETDATE()

Embed INTO io_snapshots_statistics

(snap_id,

[db_id],

[file_id],

database_name ,

physical_file_name,

Diff_Number_of_reads,

Diff_Bytes_Read,

Diff_Read_stall_time_ms,

Diff_Number_of_writes,

Diff_Bytes_written,

Diff_Write_stall_time_ms,

Diff_Read_Write_stall_ms,

size_on_disk_MB)

SELECT

```
(SELECT MAX(snap_id) FROM
io_snapshots),


db_files.database_id,


db_files.FILE_ID,


DB_NAME(db_files.database_id) AS
Database_Name,


db_files.physical_name AS
File_actual_name,


num_of_reads AS Number_of_reads,


num_of_bytes_read AS Bytes_Read,


io_stall_read_ms AS Read_time_stall_ms,


num_of_writes AS Number_of_writes,
```

```sql
	num_of_bytes_written AS Bytes_written,


	io_stall_write_ms AS Write_time_stall_ms,


	io_stall AS Read_Write_stall_ms,


	size_on_disk_bytes/POWER(1024,2) AS
size_on_disk_MB


FROM


sys.dm_io_virtual_file_stats(NULL,NULL)
dm_io_vf_stats ,


sys.master_files db_files


WHERE


db_files.database_id =
dm_io_vf_stats.database_id
```

Furthermore, db_files.[file_id] = dm_io_vf_stats.[file_id];

SET NOCOUNT OFF

END

GO

The second SP (usp_compare_io_stats_snaps) demonstrates the distinction between two previews and can be run a few ways:

1. If you don't go in any parameter values it will analyze the last two previews that were made

2. If you go in just the beginning preview ID then it will contrast that depiction and the last preview

3. Lastly, you can go in a beginning preview ID and a closure depiction ID to think about any two eras

- The Second Procedure.

Make PROC
[dbo].[usp_compare_io_stats_snaps]

(@start_snap_ID INT = NULL,

@end_snap_ID INT = NULL)

AS

Announce @end_snp INT

Announce @start_snp INT

Start

```
SET NOCOUNT ON


In the event that (@end_snap_ID IS NULL)


SELECT @end_snp = MAX(snap_id) FROM
io_snapshots


ELSE SET @end_snp = @end_snap_ID


In the event that (@start_snap_ID IS
NULL)


SELECT @start_snp = @end_snp - 1


ELSE SET @start_snp = @start_snap_ID


SELECT


CONVERT(VARCHAR(12),S.snapshot_crea
tion_date,101) AS snapshot_creation_date,
```

A.database_name,

A.physical_file_name,

A.size_on_disk_MB,

A.Diff_Number_of_reads -
B.Diff_Number_of_reads AS
Diff_Number_of_reads,

A.Diff_Bytes_read - B.Diff_Bytes_read AS
Diff_Bytes_read,

A.Diff_Read_stall_time_ms -
B.Diff_Read_stall_time_ms AS
Diff_Read_stall_time_ms,

A.Diff_Number_of_writes -
B.Diff_Number_of_writes AS
Diff_Number_of_writes,

A.Diff_Bytes_written -
B.Diff_Bytes_written AS
Diff_Bytes_written,

A.Diff_Write_stall_time_ms -
B.Diff_Write_stall_time_ms AS
Diff_Write_stall_time_ms,

A.Diff_Read_Write_stall_ms -
B.Diff_Read_Write_stall_ms AS
Diff_Read_Write_stall_ms ,

DATEDIFF (hh,S1.snapshot_creation_date,
S.snapshot_creation_date) AS
Diff_time_hours

FROM

io_snapshots S ,

io_snapshots S1,

io_snapshots_statistics A ,

io_snapshots_statistics B

WHERE

S.snap_id = @end_snp AND

S.snap_id = A.snap_id AND

B.snap_id = @start_snp AND

A.[db_id] = B.[db_id] AND
A.[file_id] = B.[file_id] AND

S1.snap_id = @start_snp AND

S1.snap_id = B.snap_id

Arrange BY
A.database_name,

A.physical_file_name

SET NOCOUNT OFF

END

GO

After information has been gathered utilizing the primary SP, the second SP would be utilized to look at the distinctions. The yield would look something like the underneath pictures (the pictures were broken into two sections to make it simpler to peruse).

We can see the season of the last depiction, the database, the physical record, the contrasts between the details that were gathered and the distinction in hours between the two previews.

Next Steps

- Create the two tables and put away systems in the scripts above and start gathering measurements.

- Create a SQL Agent occupation to run usp_io_vf_stats_snap technique on an every day or hourly premise.

- After no less than two insights accumulations, you can execute usp_compare_io_stats_snaps

- Check the outcome to see where the I/O bottlenecks are and attempt to load adjust the movement on the documents by isolating them into at least two records or moving records to various drives.

SQL Server sys.dm_os_wait_stats DMV Queries

Issue

I get so baffled when attempting to figure out where to begin when a client comes to me and lets me know that "the database is moderate". Propelling Performance Monitor and running a follow in Profiler is wasteful. Unless I realize what I'm searching for in any case it's difficult to limited things down utilizing those devices! Do you have any recommendations for rapidly figuring out whether I ought to take a gander at CPU, Memory, or I/O issues without the needle v. sheaf difficulty that accompanies jumping into Perfmon and Profiler?

Arrangement

There is unquestionably a superior alternative to rapidly figuring out where you ought to spend your execution tuning assets on while experiencing a "moderate database". It's additionally connected with my most loved SQL Server subject: Dynamic Management Views. There is a particular DMV that you can rapidly inquiry to figure out whether you're managing CPU, Memory, or Disk (I/O) issues: sys.dm_os_wait_stats. Each time SQL Server is compelled to sit tight for an asset it records the hold up. Yes, much the same as all your exes, SQL Server holds resentment too! You can *q*uestion this posting of hold up example by means of the sys.dm_os_wait_stats DMV. The section list for that DMV is demonstrated as follows:

• wait_type - the sort of hold up being experienced, the present rundown of hold up sorts is accessible from Microsoft here. There are presently 201 hold up sorts in SQL Server 2005; 485 in SQL Server 2008 as of SP1.

• waiting_tasks_count - the combined number of assignments that have enlisted this hold up since the last time SQL Server administrations were restarted.

• wait_time_ms - the combined measure of sit tight time enlisted for all undertakings experiencing this kind of hold up since the SQL Server administrations were restarted.

• max_wait_time_ms - the most extreme sit tight time for any of the assignments experiencing this hold up since last SQL Server benefit restart.

• signal_wait_time_ms - the measure of time, in milliseconds, any demand held up in the wake of being flagged that the asset was liberated, until a specialist was alloted to handle the demand. A high flag hold up time is characteristic of CPU issues in that the string still needed to sit tight for CPU task even after the asset being attended to was arranged for.

I made say over that the data is total for this DMV. This data is held in store. It will be lost/reset upon administrations restart. On the off chance that you need to keep up history for this metadata you might need to consider holding on the data in a physical table. More about that later in this tip however.

All in all, what does the information from this DMV resemble? We should see a portion of the outcomes based upon a basic SELECT *... inquiry:


```
SELECT * FROM sys.dm_os_wait_stats;
```


Taking a gander at the specimen yield you'll see that outcomes are returned for each wait_type, paying little mind to regardless of whether there were any total errands that attended to assets for that particular sort. You can likewise observe that secure sorts are incorporated into the yield of sys.dm_os_wait_stats. A general question of this sort doesn't generally let us know much however. It's alternate things we can do with this DMV that are telling.

Glenn Berry, in his part on DMVs in the late MVP Deep Dive Book, had an incredible inquiry that uses sys.dm_os_wait_stats. I've taken that inquiry and adjusted it somewhat for my utilization to get a preview of holds up in rate shape at the present point in time. By making a typical table expression to fabricate a Waits table you can sift through unessential hold up sorts and afterward take a gander at a posting of simply those holds up that include the top N% (for this situation 95%) of the attends to the SQL Server case:

```
WITH Waits AS

(

SELECT

wait_type,

wait_time_ms/1000. AS wait_time_s,

100. * wait_time_ms/SUM(wait_time_ms)
OVER() AS pct,

ROW_NUMBER() OVER(ORDER BY
wait_time_ms DESC) AS rn
```

```
FROM sys.dm_os_wait_stats


WHERE wait_type


NOT IN


('CLR_SEMAPHORE',
'LAZYWRITER_SLEEP',
'RESOURCE_QUEUE',


'SLEEP_TASK', 'SLEEP_SYSTEMTASK',
'SQLTRACE_BUFFER_FLUSH', 'WAITFOR',


'CLR_AUTO_EVENT',
'CLR_MANUAL_EVENT')


) - sift through extra unessential holds up


SELECT W1.wait_type,
```

```
CAST(W1.wait_time_s AS DECIMAL(12,
2)) AS wait_time_s,


CAST(W1.pct AS DECIMAL(12, 2)) AS pct,


CAST(SUM(W2.pct) AS DECIMAL(12, 2))
AS running_pct


FROM Waits AS W1


Inward JOIN Waits AS W2 ON W2.rn <=
W1.rn


Assemble BY W1.rn,


W1.wait_type,


W1.wait_time_s,


W1.pct
```

HAVING SUM(W2.pct) - W1.pct < 95; -
rate edge;

For this situation you'll see that since the
last SQL Server administrations restart,
I'm essentially managing
ASYNC_NETWORK_IO and OLEDB waits
on my SQL Server case. I know there to be
issues with a particular application on my
server that causes these holds up because
of performing line by-column handling of
SQL clump comes about sets came back to
the application. The
SOS_SCHEDULER_YIELD hold up happens
at whatever point an assignment presents
its place in line to permit another
procedure to keep running in its stead. It
is demonstrative of CPU issues that may
should be tended to. Particular holds up
will point you toward where to center
your tuning assets on the grounds that
the reason for specific holds up are
credited specifically to CPU, memory, or
I/O. The PAGEIOLATCH_... holds up are
demonstrative of I/O issues, as is
WRITELOG. CXPACKET is a marker of
holds up because of questions going
parallel and running over various CPU
centers. I emphatically recommend taking
after the Microsoft CSS Team's blog and
perusing through the *q*uantity of sections

connected with sit tight sorts for the ceaseless advancement of exactness tuning utilizing sys.dm_os_wait_stats.

The vital thing to recollect is that the measurements for the sections returned while questioning sys.dm_os_wait_stats is total. Like all Dynamic Management Object data these qualities amass after some time and are wiped-clean at a SQL Server benefit restart. This is the reason I said holding on the data in a static table on a committed managerial database situated on each oversaw SQL Server example. You can then question the data only for the period between the last two details accumulations. I utilize a SQL Server Agent work that runs hourly to continue the data to the static table. You could either run the code physically when fancied or plan as works best in your association. The question is lightweight, not by any means excessively perceptible on a nicely estimated server. The format script beneath will permit you to do only that. Take note of that the rest of the scripts in this post utilize layout documentation. CTRL+SHIFT+M in SQL Server Management Studio will give a frame to enter parameter values that are right for your surroundings.

Utilize [<database_name,,Foo>];

- Create table to hold on hold up details data:

Make TABLE <table_schema_name,,dbo>.<table_name,, dm_os_wait_stats>

(

[wait_type] [nvarchar](60) NOT NULL,

[waiting_tasks_count] [bigint] NOT NULL,

[wait_time_ms] [bigint] NOT NULL,

[max_wait_time_ms] [bigint] NOT NULL,

[signal_wait_time_ms] [bigint] NOT NULL,

[capture_time] [datetime] NOT NULL,

[increment_id] [int] NOT NULL

);

Modify TABLE
<table_schema_name,,dbo>.<table_name,,
dm_os_wait_stats>

Include DEFAULT (GETDATE()) FOR
[capture_time];

- Insert hold up details data in a
datestamped arrange for later
questioning:

Proclaim @DT DATETIME ;

SET @DT = GETDATE() ;

Proclaim @increment_id INT;

SELECT @increment_id =
MAX(increment_id) + 1 FROM
<table_schema_name,,dbo>.<table_name,,
dm_os_wait_stats>;

SELECT @increment_id =
ISNULL(@increment_id, 1)

Embed INTO
<database_name,,Foo>.<table_schema_na
me,,dbo>.<table_name,,dm_os_wait_stats>

([wait_type], [waiting_tasks_count],
[wait_time_ms], [max_wait_time_ms],

[signal_wait_time_ms], [capture_time], [increment_id])

SELECT [wait_type],
[waiting_tasks_count], [wait_time_ms],
[max_wait_time_ms],

[signal_wait_time_ms], @DT,
@increment_id

FROM sys.dm_os_wait_stats;

The accompanying data would be held on to the physical table of your picking. On the off chance that utilizing the defaults as a part of the format it would be Foo.dbo.dm_os_wait_stats. Take note of how it makes and increment_id and datestamp for the information gathered:

At that point you can run a question like this and just view tallies coming about because of late movement - not action over days, months, weeks, and so on (trailing sections expelled from screen shot for space concerns):

- Return continued data from table

Utilize [<database_name,,Foo>];

Announce @max_increment_id INT

- - - - -

- Determine latest increment_id

- - - - -

SELECT @max_increment_id =
MAX(increment_id)

FROM
<table_schema_name,,dbo>.<table_name,,
dm_os_wait_stats>

- - - - -

- Present Waits comes about for period

- - - - -

SELECT DOWS1.wait_type,

(DOWS1.waiting_tasks_count -
DOWS2.waiting_tasks_count) AS
[waiting_tasks_count],

(DOWS1.wait_time_ms -
DOWS2.wait_time_ms) AS [wait_time_ms],

DOWS1.max_wait_time_ms,

(DOWS1.signal_wait_time_ms -
DOWS2.signal_wait_time_ms) AS
[signal_wait_time_ms],

DATEDIFF(ms, DOWS2.capture_time,
DOWS1.capture_time) AS
[elapsed_time_ms],

DOWS1.capture_time AS
[last_time_stamp], DOWS2.capture_time
AS [previous_time_stamp]

FROM

(

SELECT wait_type, waiting_tasks_count,
wait_time_ms, max_wait_time_ms,

signal_wait_time_ms, capture_time,
increment_id

FROM
<table_schema_name,,dbo>.<table_name,,
dm_os_wait_stats>

WHERE increment_id =
@max_increment_id

)AS DOWS1

Inward JOIN

(

SELECT wait_type, waiting_tasks_count, wait_time_ms, max_wait_time_ms,

signal_wait_time_ms, capture_time, increment_id

FROM <table_schema_name,,dbo>.<table_name,, dm_os_wait_stats>

WHERE increment_id = (@max_increment_id - 1)

)AS DOWS2 ON DOWS1.wait_type = DOWS2.wait_type

WHERE (DOWS1.wait_time_ms - DOWS2.wait_time_ms) > 0

```
/*


This can in fact be wiped out on the
grounds that we're not continuing these
holds up:


Furthermore, DOWS1.wait_type NOT IN


('CLR_SEMAPHORE',
'LAZYWRITER_SLEEP',
'RESOURCE_QUEUE',


'SLEEP_TASK', 'SLEEP_SYSTEMTASK',
'SQLTRACE_BUFFER_FLUSH', 'WAITFOR',


'CLR_AUTO_EVENT',
'CLR_MANUAL_EVENT')


*/


Arrange BY (DOWS1.wait_time_ms -
DOWS2.wait_time_ms) DESC;
```

At long last, you could re-instrument the prior top N% holds up inquiry to look at simply the latest hold up details action from the continued table as exhibited underneath. You can use this procedure (fabricating a CTE contrasting deltas for simply the action gathered since the last two surveying time frames) to retrofit any inquiry you find online for breaking down outcomes from sys.dm_os_wait_stats.

- wait_stats as rate only for current gathering period:

Utilize [<database_name,,Foo>];

Announce @max_increment_id INT

- - - - -

- Determine latest increment_id

- - - - -

```
SELECT @max_increment_id =
MAX(increment_id)


FROM
<table_schema_name,,dbo>.<table_name,,
dm_os_wait_stats>;



- - - - -



- Present Waits comes about for period

- - - - -



WITH Waits AS



(



SELECT DOWS1.wait_type,



((DOWS1.wait_time_ms -
DOWS2.wait_time_ms)/1000) AS
[wait_time_s],
```

```sql
100. * (DOWS1.wait_time_ms -
DOWS2.wait_time_ms)/SUM(DOWS1.wait
_time_ms - DOWS2.wait_time_ms) OVER()
AS pct,


ROW_NUMBER() OVER(ORDER BY
(DOWS1.wait_time_ms -
DOWS2.wait_time_ms) DESC) AS rn


FROM


(


SELECT wait_type, waiting_tasks_count,
wait_time_ms, max_wait_time_ms,


signal_wait_time_ms, capture_time,
increment_id
FROM
<table_schema_name,,dbo>.<table_name,,
dm_os_wait_stats>
```

```
WHERE increment_id =
@max_increment_id


)AS DOWS1


Internal JOIN


(


SELECT wait_type, waiting_tasks_count,
wait_time_ms, max_wait_time_ms,


signal_wait_time_ms, capture_time,
increment_id


FROM
<table_schema_name,,dbo>.<table_name,,
dm_os_wait_stats>


WHERE increment_id =
(@max_increment_id - 1)
```

```sql
)AS DOWS2 ON DOWS1.wait_type =
DOWS2.wait_type


WHERE (DOWS1.wait_time_ms -
DOWS2.wait_time_ms) > 0


)


SELECT W1.wait_type,


CAST(W1.wait_time_s AS DECIMAL(12,
2)) AS wait_time_s,


CAST(W1.pct AS DECIMAL(12, 2)) AS pct,


CAST(SUM(W2.pct) AS DECIMAL(12, 2))
AS running_pct


FROM Waits AS W1
```

Internal JOIN Waits AS W2 ON W2.rn <= W1.rn

Amass BY W1.rn,

W1.wait_type,

W1.wait_time_s,

W1.pct

HAVING SUM(W2.pct) - W1.pct < 95; - rate limit;

Conclusion

Thank you again for downloading this book!

I hope this book was able to help you to UNDERSTAND Presently, how about we make a put away technique that has a select proclamation utilizing script-3 beneath. After the SP has been made, execute the put away proc dbo.

Finally, if you enjoyed this book, then I'd like to ask you for a favor, would you be kind enough to leave a review for this book on Amazon? It'd be greatly appreciated!

Thank you and good luck!

I truly do appreciate it!

Best Wishes,

Lee Maxwell

www.ingramcontent.com/pod-product-compliance
Lightning Source LLC
Chambersburg PA
CBHW071158050326
40689CB00011B/2160